CU01052364

Fossil Sunshine

BY THE SAME AUTHOR

Still This Need (Heaventree Press, 2009)

FOSSIL SUNSHINE

Michael McKimm

First published in 2013 by
Worple Press
Achill Sound, 2b Dry Hill Road
Tonbridge
Kent TN9 1LX.
www.worplepress.co.uk

© Copyright Michael McKimm

The moral right of the author has been asserted in accordance with
the Copyrights, Designs and Patents Act of 1988. All rights reserved.

Cover image by the author

No part of this work covered by the copyright thereon may be
reproduced or used in any means – graphic, electronic, or mechanical,
including copying, recording, taping, or information storage or
retrieval systems – without written permission of the publisher.

Printed by imprintdigital
Upton Pyne, Exeter
www.imprintdigital.net

Typeset by narrator
www.narrator.me.uk
enquiries@narrator.me.uk

ISBN: 978-1-905208-20-3

Acknowledgements

Thanks to the editors of *Magma, Stravaig, The Warwick Review* and *The Wolf* where some of these poems first appeared.

I am grateful to the Arts Council England Grants for the Arts scheme for financial assistance in researching and writing these poems.

I would especially like to thank Dr Bryan Lovell, for sparking the project and for his enthusiasm, advice and support throughout.

This work has benefited from the influence and assistance of a great many people. I thank in particular Dr Mike Horne and the many geologists I met in Yorkshire, Dr Andy Woods and researchers at the BP Institute, Cambridge, Dr Andrew Leonard, Peter Carpenter, Penelope Shuttle, Anna Kirk-Smith, my colleagues at The Geological Society.

Finally, thanks, as always, to Zachary Lamdin.

Contents

Tertiary Basalts

Crow black, slick as onions, or walk-on-nails
tough for the child with his bamboo crab net.
True basalt country. In summer, when you put
your hand to it, you could swear to feel the heat

of its forging, could believe it would burst
like bubbling tarmac. Walking east round
Runkerry Point, sheep spread on scatch-grass,
rumps inked red, the rocks were blacker than ever:

cauldron and demon, kindred spirits of the dark arts.
Headlands competed. The humped Stookans
and the Grand Causeway. A thick burnt red
running through like a layer of jam: interbasaltic

laterite, the field guide says. New words
for old familiars. Today, where the rope-bridge
swings over banded ash and basalt bomb, land
opens south as remnant plug and cinder cone

of the North Atlantic's slow volcanic rosary,
its full-on carbon dump that made the oceans boil.
These, my gnarled, unruly basalts, tumbling
from the cliff to break the waves

the way I used to think they always would.
They gave to me more pictures than the clouds.
I close the book, put my hand to a large loose
pathway boulder, try to feel the heat of its forging.

Abstract from a Conference 1

Coal, oil, gas – let's call these ancient,
rather than contemporary, sunshine.

Sunshine we sought with our intelligence
and drive: genies hidden in the earth.

Fossil sunshine, animal and plant long dead.
Seeping from the ground. Exposed in cliffs.

Not the sort we knew as heat on skin,
that gave us night's black signal to rest,

day's light permit to move and work.
That contemporary beacon for our crops:

contemporary as in constant, as in modern,
as in still here. Is it possible, a soft

landing for civilisation? We were smart.
How smart do we now want to be?

Holderness Boulder Clay

January. Midnight buffetings reveal
Baltic amber, black flints, quartz,
a fencepost hanging from a whip
of wire, and plastic drainage pipes
like pillarbox guns, their artillery
of soapsuds and effluent. The sea
knows no other path but February,
waves coaxing new erratics
right through March, glacier-scored
conglomerates, jasper, Weardale
limestone, and molluscs, ostracods,
fish teeth, fish scales, fish spines, and then it's
April, the pounding ocean undercuts
where pebbles milled a cave
and out into the water flows silt, clay,
Devil's toenails plucky as iambics,
fossil wood as hard as lumps
of coal. On the verge the caravans
roll back; then just like that another
two feet fall. May and June bring
sand martins, burrowing above
the latest slump, hundreds nipping
grasses from behind the Public
Beach Conveniences, clearing bugs
before the second brood.
Soaked July, the channels fill with rain,
then scorching August, creaking
in the air, a good half metre crumbles
with a Scafell thud. A man out
with his trowel, checking silt grains
on his tongue, measures with his eyes

the tide's new reach, the Millennium
defences now they're breached.
And something else he lifts up from the sand;
a finely polished double-yellow line.
September sees a balmy orange sun
and the fields above stripped bare
by rolling combines; the upper ridge
dries out; mud-balls loll like peppered
steaks at the lowest tide. Winds work
through October, bring up
gobstoppers of granite, sandstone,
Norwegian porphyry, carnelian;
bring up ammonites, gastropods,
tight-nippled cirripedes; bring
another layer from the cliff face,
enough to show the light to agate,
and garnet, and gneiss, and November.
A huge swell takes the life out
of a groyne, saws non-stop for days
at beds of clay. And that's
two full metres gone before December.

The Bindon Landslide

When the earth began to move, cracks daggering
the chalk cliff path, they thought nothing of it,
went home to their beds, the landlord's Christmas
whisky still hot on their breath, bellies happy
with sweetmeats and pickle. They slept with deep,
dark dreams of the day, of the horse buckling
in the limestone quarry and heavy hods cutting
their shoulders, then darker dreams of sulphur
and sinkholes, dank pools of bitumen, rivers
of leachate, pipelines, convoys, midnight tankers,
and the sea roaring, agitated, an intolerable
stench that woke them, their tenements rending
and sinking, the moon in the window entirely ajar,
fissures gaping, they'd say, like the mouth of hell.

Riptide

If I am photographing a disaster, it's a slow, intentional, incremental one
  – Edward Burtynsky

As slow as this: the sudden loss of suction –
what's incubated in the depths now free,
swollen, then breathing, breathing
and quickening in water, but slowly, salt
dark taste, a dim light, a cautious rise,
slowly, slower than before, sneaking past
dispersant, escaping atomization, finding
a way, a slow and simple tear at the seams,
the drag eddying north – brackish
Mississippi – then quick cold wall of ocean,
blue on blue, nowhere to go, the water
veined and hard as tattooed leather, you
a reef – you some lost mammalian mass
washed in by hurricane, eating everything.

Abstract from a Conference 2

For me it dates to farming,
first forest clearances by fire,
smoothing out the land we re-named fields.
Tillage, shifting cultivations.
Knowledge of crops and the intricate seasons.

Survivalists, stewards of the biosphere,
from nothing we grew. Slowly learned
to tame the kyne, surrounded our homes
with loose thickets of breeding-pens.
Walked behind manure's bright stink

as we thought of what to plant
and for how long. Doused the soil.
Moved and changed it.
Barren swathes that would not root
until we cropped, re-cropped, dammed rivers,

sliced channels, thought of ourselves –
and where was the harm in that? –
as the mighty river's arteries flowed past.

Abstract from a Conference 3

It's as simple as sediment flux:
what we've moved from land to water.

Let's cover the basics: deforestation, fallow lands,
tilling, terracing, irrigation systems, subsurface

water extraction, mining, transportation systems,
waterway re-plumbing, reservoir interception,

groynes, jetties, seawalls, breakwaters, harbours,
warfare that magnifies many of the above

for a duration that extends beyond the period
of combat, dissipation in the frozen north.

I'm afraid it's too soon to tell the impact
of sea-floor trawling on the continental shelf.

Pipeline

Out of Hardisty, four feet up, zig-zagging
through conifers, flexing and thinking, the tiniest tilt,
leaving the landscape of smokestacks and bitumen,
Alberta highlands clutched in pack ice,
southering, steadily, not slowing, not quickening,
kinking past farmyards, barnsteads and combines,
crossing the railroad, saying hello to Oyen,
so close that its night hum is the dreamsong
of townsfolk, providing upwards of five hundred jobs,
and then a slow left turn
and it's into Saskatchewan, fields flaring yellow
or ploughed into tweeds, Deer Forks and Happyland,
Mirv Creek, Excelsior, nothing but flat now,
coasting the highway, Humvees and truck stops,
log loads and plant hire, kids slapping kids
in the back of Corollas, excited and nervy
for their week in Regina,
Regina the heart of the spider, sending its train legs
to Strasbourg, Camp Dundrum, Lumsden
and Weyburn – here it just sneaks past, nothing to
freight trains, on again with its stealth,
its glimpsed-through-the-tree-banks, its water or
phone lines, its surely-just-cables –

without even a pit stop it's pierced Manitoba,
steady trajectory, knows where it's going,
till just south of Lake Manitoba's black liver, a sudden
right angle, a little pick up in speed,
Grey and Dufferin, rippling past Carman,
Roland then Morden, there it is, it's the border,
the lowlands and prairies of warm North Dakota,
taking vast empty stretches, hay fields, dry wheat,
a glint in the eye for the Spirit Lake Sioux,
down through the sunflowers, the soybeans
and barley, sugar beets, corn, oats and potatoes,
without noticing difference the other Dakota,
making the most of the James River valley
before the land rises going into Nebraska,
stressing in heat in this drought-hit summer,
over the top of the Ogallala Aquifer,
for a good thousand miles, soon to be more –
its ticking and tensing alerts the odd muskrat,
at night time it's floodlit by curious eyes,
raccoons, timid bobcats, mink and black bear,
the yipping coyote swimming in fireflies –

and still on its journey, a left at Steele City,
touching down in north Kansas for barely an hour,
into Missouri, whistling Dixie – kissing the cleft
of the Mississippi – then sunny St. Charles,
not even a run up, over the water
to west Illinois, Granite City, Wood River,
a first refresh and slowdown, then off again east,
through Madison, Washington, Jefferson, Clinton,
past the strip mall and Java House and school canteen,
past further full fields, ready for harvest,
past the Eldon Hazlet State Park,
to the Pakota Terminal, the terminal stop.

The Saw Pit Road

A first break after five full days of rain:
gum boots sinking into Bagshot mud,
the forest cool in corrugated light.
A furtive smell of long logs neatly stacked
beside the road, December felled, their ends
ringed distances of summers wet and dry,
the odd black smudge of pest or airborne threat
locked in like memory in each bark brain.
We find an oak tree girdered at its back,
its branches thick with dark fern epiphytes;
blow-ins, nesting high above the floods,
flared leaves reaching for the white-bleached sky.
A monolith, the studded oak distends:
its belly heaves against its metal corset.

Abstract from a Conference 4

worked ground		
worked ground	*engineered excavation*	
worked ground	engineered excavation	*canal cutting*
worked ground	engineered excavation	*artificial pond/lake*
worked ground	engineered excavation	*rail cutting*
worked ground	engineered excavation	*road cutting*
worked ground	*mineral extraction*	
worked ground	mineral extraction	*quarry (hard rock)*
worked ground	mineral extraction	*pit (superficial deposits)*
made ground		
made ground	*engineered embankment*	
made ground	engineered embankment	*flood defence embankment*
made ground	engineered embankment	*rail embankment*
made ground	engineered embankment	*road embankment*
made ground	engineered embankment	*reservoir embankment*
made ground	engineered embankment	*screen embankment*
made ground	*waste tip*	
made ground	waste tip	*mine waste tip (colliery)*
infilled ground		

infilled ground (undivided): worked ground (undivided) and made ground (undivided)

infilled ground: worked ground (undivided) filled by mine waste tip (colliery)

infilled ground: pit (superficial deposit) filled by made ground (undivided)

infilled ground: pit (superficial deposit) filled by mine waste tip (colliery)

landscaped ground	
landscaped ground	*landscaping for site formation*
landscaped ground	*landscaping for recreational purposes*

Laosciadia Planus

No sooner had Stuart arrived than he found a fossil sea sponge. It looked to me no different from the other smaller boulders on the beach, and of course I'd been looking for the wrong thing entirely: the sponge lay under the skin of chalk-dust like a condom under its wrapper. Holding the rock in his left hand, his left leg supported on a boulder, Stuart brought his hammer down to crack it as you might crack a coconut, though of course Yorkshire chalk is harder than coconut. He turned it, hammered. Turned, hammered again. Soon we had to stand some metres back as bits of chalk – fingernails, marbles, skin-flints – spun randomly to hit us. When he'd got as near as he could without it breaking, he handed me the sea-sponge-squatted rock. *Laosciadia Planus*. I weighed it in my hand. On top it was a rough bowl, thick lipped, with green mossy fungus rubbed around its edge and into crevices. In places it was dimpled like a golf ball. Underneath, where a chunk had come away with Stuart's last blow, sprouted the rust corona of its stem. I looked down coast towards the amusements at Bridlington. The road train. Pitch and Putt. Imagine it ocean, tropically stormed. Sea conifers, angiosperms. The whole place electric with reptiles. The sponge in my hand anchored to the sea floor by this small coin of stem, its everyday sway, filtering water for food. There's a trick to cracking Yorkshire chalk, I heard Stuart say, though I failed to write it down or even listen.

Field Notes

Bempton Cliffs

Beneath the surface, stretching for a mile,
the huge chalk platform's grinded into pits
by wave-chucked boulders and the pelted gravels.
Add to this the way the platform fits
with the western end of a major step
in the North Sea, and conditions are ideal:
the forces on the water mean it's kept
refreshed and rich in nutrients, a field
of algae thrives in wave-cut crevices,
anemones and hybrids court with fists
of sea urchins, piddock's interstices.
It's the southern limit of the kelp forest.
And up above, where gannets collect,
a thatch of wild flowers grows, guano-flecked.

Selwicks Bay

Like veins of fat in a hock of ham
fault lines score down heaved chalk cliffs
and across the thick shore platform.
The flints are uniform, and calcite clefts
indicate the brecciated crush zone
occurring to the south of the west-east
latitude of tectonic disturbance.
It's highly complex, to say the least.
But there's a rhythm in the chalk –
soft and harder beds, nodules, wispy marls,
alternating flints – regular as clocks
that mark a record of Cretaceous cycles:
the whole Earth's orbit accurately ranged,
these frequencies a pace-maker for change.

Danes Dyke

We are waiting for results from Sheffield
on the sample taken from the horizontal
borehole. Initially we thought the gravels
could be correlatives of interglacials
found further west - do you follow? -
but now we read in their significance
the movement of the North Sea Lobe
of the last ice sheet in eastern England.
Freeze and thaw has worked the sediments.
On top of these are laminated muds
and rippled sands, suggesting ice was present
to the south. But we're not wizened Druids
with hazel wands. This is just our impulse.
We're eagerly awaiting the results.

Sewerby

We take a sample from the buried cliff:
raised beach shingle, chalk, the Skipsea Till,
coarse and imbricated gravels. We lift
small cupfuls to the microscope, label
hippopotamus, hyena, straight-tusked
elephant, bison, deer and water vole.
We sort the flints from temperate molluscs,
wild erratics found in kettle holes.
Thermoluminescence dates the blown sand
to a period mid-Ipswichian.
Going further back, we see then how the land
in fact curved west away from Bridlington,
and where we took the rocks, the cliff we walked,
did not exist, was low Cretaceous chalk.

Abstract from a Conference 5

Know the oceans
are being altered

the nature of the seafloor
will change

cream-coloured
calcium carbonate

dissolved to darker clays

Oil Field

You'd have thought that we were headed
into wilderness, crossing the frost-still marsh
through the forest's early cataract of light.
Our quiet coach was clocked by long-horned bulls,
ghost-white in clearances and shaded leas.
And even when we caught first sight
of fencing and the nodding donkeys,
they somehow looked so incidental, sparse
amongst the trees, the distant yachts at Poole.

We parked, disembarked. The air was sent
our steamed October breath. We smelled just pine.
The security guard yelled "No photography".
We walked up through the forest in a line
then gathered on a ridge above the fence
to watch the heaving wells, their duck and pull,
their slow lament, or maybe stoic dream –
three kings, commanding and benevolent.
How calm it was, the wind sock hanging limp.

We stayed out of long grass, avoiding ticks,
and perhaps it was too cold for dreaded
wood ants to materialize. My jeans were stuck
in brambles where I plucked a blackberry.
And still the only noise – apart from science,
apart from average stats – was the beam pump's
gentle purr, like an antique Singer threaded
through with jet, working with a rhythm
you would never think so peaceful or so clean.

Carbon Capture and Storage

after Lovell

by Ermine Street
the straight A10
a new ploughed field
left foot crunches
85Ma chalk right foot
55Ma pebble beds
rounded flints
hard cement
puddingstone

*

a proof
pebbly beach
Hertford-on-Sea
uncemented white fine sand
silica bound
by intense warming
Paleocene-Eocene Thermal Maximum
boundary of an epoch
carbon dump

*

a coach pulls up at Kimmeridge
caked wall
lonely nodding donkey
a proof
North Sea oil
migrates through pores
fractures
overlying mud
source   reservoir   trap   seal

*

penalties in Earth Court
unfinished business
separation
compression and dehydration
or gasification
reservoir refilling
pipe   dream
as if people mattered
if they fund it   we will fit it

*

by Ermine Street the straight A10
a new ploughed field

The Year Without a Summer

Early, early, the magic hour.
His hand floats, tickles wheat's
antennae, strokes ribs and plucks
one fine long ear up into the blue
rim of daylight. The same part
of the main field every year,
big John Deeres behind him
ticking over, men done with breakfast
in their cabs, a beard of spikes
thrown to the wind, thumbs pressed
between the spine, kernels brought
with a stiff sniff to his nose.

He smells the history of the field.
Those pictures of hired help
heaving grainy stooks into their hands.
And further back, what too is
passed down like a photograph:
his namesake gaunt and sunken
in a lea three deep with snow: July 1816,
the year without a summer.
Nothing in the till, or choice of fields,
nothing in the timing of the crop.
He closes wheat dust in his palms,
raises them together with a prayer.

Abstract from a Conference: Plenary

We might consider this:
balloons of sulphur –

about the size of basket
blimps tethered

at fairs – balloons of burning
particles sent into

the stratosphere – or even
this: fixed artillery

firing sulphur from
the surface – I'm deadly

serious – sulphur to reflect
the sun, to cool

the climate, to give us time.
We could even try it

with a trillion
wisp-thin mirrors.

Or we might want
to start a nuclear winter –

we'd do this by releasing
particles of soot –

this is actually the cheaper
option, and less messy.

You don't believe me.
Well I'm deadly serious –

this is where we are.
This we must consider.

Notes

'Tertiary Basalts': 55 million years ago CO_2 released into the atmosphere by the opening of the North Atlantic coincided with an intense period of global warming (the 55Ma event).

'Abstract from a Conference': see *The Anthropocene: A New Epoch of Geological Time? [meeting held on] Wednesday 11th May [2011 at The Geological Society of London, Burlington House]: abstract book and programme.*

'The Bindon Landslide': Bindon, Dorset, Christmas Day 1839.

'Oil Field': Wytch Farm Oil Field, in Dorset, is the UK's largest onshore oil field.

'Carbon Capture and Storage': see Lovell, B. *Challenged by Carbon: the Oil Industry and Climate Change* (Cambridge University Press, 2009).

'A Year Without a Summer': the summer of 1816 saw dramatic temperature reductions and heavy snowfall in the northern hemisphere due to ash from major volcanic eruptions.

'Holderness Boulder Clay' is for Mike Horne; 'Laosciadia Planus' is for Stuart Jones; 'Oil Field' is for Bryan Lovell.